COMICS

Genius Birds

CROWS
Genius Birds

KYLA VANDERKLUGT

:01

First Second
New York

For Maxwell, who loved birds,
and for Merlin, who loved to eat them.

First Second

Published by First Second
First Second is an imprint of Roaring Brook Press,
a division of Holtzbrinck Publishing Holdings Limited Partnership
120 Broadway, New York, NY 10271

Don't miss your next favorite book from First Second! For the latest updates
go to firstsecondnewsletter.com and sign up for our enewsletter.

Library of Congress Control Number: 2019930674

Hardcover ISBN: 978-1-62672-803-5
Paperback ISBN: 978-1-62672-802-8

Our books may be purchased in bulk for promotional, educational, or business use. Please
contact your local bookseller or the Macmillan Corporate and Premium Sales Department
at (800) 221-7945 ext. 5442 or by email at MacmillanSpecialMarkets@macmillan.com.

First edition, 2020
Edited by Dave Roman
Cover design by Andrew Arnold and Molly Johanson
Interior book design by Laura Berry
Crows consultant: Kevin J. McGowan, Cornell Lab of Ornithology

Printed in China by Toppan Leefung Printing Ltd., Dongguan City, Guangdong Province

Penciled, inked, and colored in Adobe Photoshop.

Paperback: 10 9 8 7 6

Hardcover: 10 9 8 7 6 5 4 3 2

Most days I'm sure I have the best job in the world. Not only do I get to work with terrific students, but I also get to learn from the truly amazing birds that are featured in the book you are now holding. Thanks to a great high school biology teacher who instilled in me a love of nature and science, I've been able to study crows and their close relatives (jays, nutcrackers, and ravens) for almost 40 years. During my career, I've watched these birds do many of the things you will read about. Yes, they really are as smart as chimps or even small kids! They do make tools, learn rules, speak, and even command dogs! My friend Kevin Smith actually almost lost his dog, Vampire, to a crow that famously made the rounds in Missoula, Montana. The crow was apparently raised by a person and, as they will do, learned to repeat what it must have often heard. In this case the crow approached dogs and called forth in plain English: "Here, boy, here, boy." Most dogs followed the crow's instructions, but fortunately Kevin got out to his kennel before the crow coaxed his big German shepherd away.

Crows are able to do such amazing things because they learn from personal encounters and by watching other crows. They use their sophisticated brains to remember what they've experienced and to think before they act. Sound familiar? Yes, as social beings, crows use their brains in much the same way we do. The mental ability of crows is important because it allows them to solve real problems, such as where to hide surplus food and how to coordinate the movements of their family when a predator lurks nearby. As we create cities and farms, many animals go extinct or retreat to more natural settings, but not the crow. Living close to people is not an easy task; for example, while some folks feed crows, others harass or even hunt them. Crows are able to meet this challenge because they can recognize us and remember how we've treated them in the past. I discovered this the hard way. After I captured crows and put identifying bracelets on their legs, I realized that they treated me differently. Once released, the crow would rarely approach its nest if I was watching, and sometimes the bird would aggressively dive at me and scold me with harsh calls. This made studying them tough! But it also suggested an experiment I'm glad to have done. My students and I wore caveman masks the next time we caught crows. After we released them, we tested their reactions to us when we wore the caveman masks, no masks, or different masks. The crows immediately recognized us when we wore the caveman masks, but ignored us otherwise. Now 11 years after catching those crows, they still recognize the caveman, and they've taught their kids, mates, and neighbors about the dangerous caveman, as well!

Lately, my research team has looked within the head of a crow to discover how its brain stores and recalls information about particular people. We've done this without harming the bird, by using a brain imaging technique called a PET scan. This research showed us that crows use the same parts of their brains as we do—the hippocampus and amygdala—to learn and respond to fearful events. We are continuing our brain scanning research in the hope of discovering how the crows' brains function during tool use and how they decode their rich language.

I admit that I'm pretty possessed by crows, but I'm far from alone. Crows and ravens have challenged and inspired humans for a millennia. There are raven images in Lascaux cave art! Our close and personal interactions with these birds have shaped our beliefs, arts, and language. You know what a "crowbar" is and what it means to be "ravenous," right? Given the intelligence of crows and their relatives, it's no wonder that many Native American tribes consider the crow or raven to be their creator, that the Norse god Odin was informed daily by two ravens, or that, according to the Bible, God saved his servant Elijah by commanding a raven to bring him food.

I hope you enjoy reading about these powerful birds as much as I've enjoyed studying them. As you wonder about crows, step outside and watch your local corvids. Unless you live in Antarctica, there will be a family of crows, jays, ravens, or magpies, which are guaranteed to delight you with their cleverness, varied voice, or social antics. I'll bet that spending time among your brainy bird neighbors will give you something to crow about. Just keep a careful eye on your dog.

John M. Marzluff
Professor of Wildlife Science
University of Washington

I wonder what kind of food we'll find!

What kind of food d'you think we'll find?

Don't you worry, Buddy. With a corvid conspirator like me at your side, you'll be chowing down on all your dream foods in no time.

What's a corvid?

Any bird that belongs to the "crow family" is called a corvid.

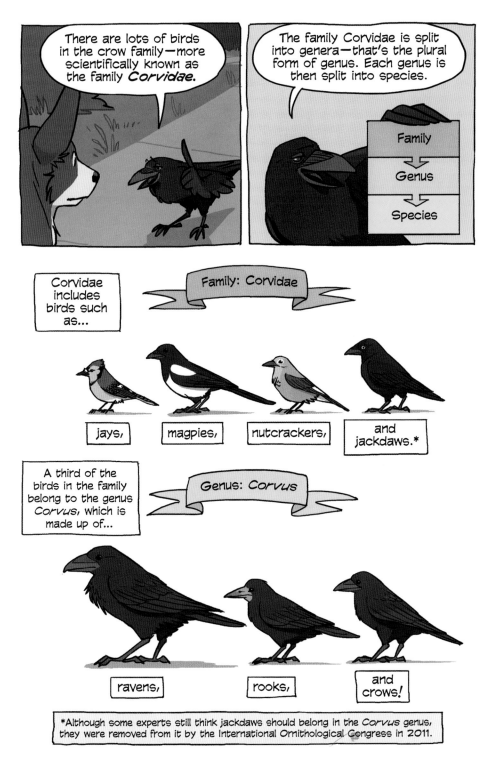

There are lots of birds in the crow family—more scientifically known as the family *Corvidae.*

The family Corvidae is split into genera—that's the plural form of genus. Each genus is then split into species.

Family
⇩
Genus
⇩
Species

Corvidae includes birds such as...

Family: Corvidae

jays,

magpies,

nutcrackers,

and jackdaws.*

A third of the birds in the family belong to the genus *Corvus,* which is made up of...

Genus: *Corvus*

ravens,

rooks,

and crows!

*Although some experts still think jackdaws should belong in the *Corvus* genus, they were removed from it by the International Ornithological Congress in 2011.

I belong to

Species:
Corvus brachyrhynchos

In plain English, that's the American crow!

Usually the smaller species in the *Corvus* genus are called crows, and the bigger species are called ravens.

Take the American crow and the common raven, for instance.

The ravens are a lot bigger.

Croak!

Caw!

Corvus brachyrhynchos / American Crow

Corvus corax / Common Raven

They also have thicker bills, longer nasal bristles, and shaggier throat feathers...

Raven

Crow

...and their tails are shaped like wedges, where a crow's is square.

Raven

Crow

Rooks are easy to tell apart because of their bald faces.

You can see their nostrils!

And they're only found in Europe and Asia.

Now, sometimes when people say "crows," they're using it as a general term for birds in the Corvidae family.

Or they might be talking about birds in the *Corvus* genus.

And sometimes they're talking about a particular species.

Crows

Crows

Crow!

But whatever they mean, you know they're talking about birds who are *really* big on brains.

Big...?

...

Is your brain really that big?

Of course it is. It's *huge!*

But you're so tiny.

How can your brain be that big?

Ah. Well, when I say it's big, I'm speaking *relatively.*

Brains are complex. Like, really complex.

And scientists still aren't sure how to accurately measure an animal's intelligence, but they have some theories.

$$\frac{EW \, (brain)}{1g} = 0.12 \left(\frac{w \, (body)}{1g} \right)^{\frac{2}{5}}$$

Some think it's the relative size of the brain.

Corvus brachyrhynchos
American Crow

Columba livia
Pigeon

Brain:Body Weight Ratio

Crow
1:50

Pigeon
1:150

A pigeon and crow are about the same size, but a crow's brain is much larger compared to its body.

When an animal has a larger brain than expected compared to similar animals, the difference between the actual and expected brain size is called the EQ— or if you want to be fancy, the *encephalization quotient.*

Crows have a much higher EQ than pigeons, since a crow's brain is surprisingly large for its body size.

In fact, a crow's EQ is equal to many primates. Our brains are relatively the same size as a chimpanzee's!

EQ

EQ

The forebrain is where the *prefrontal cortex*, or PFC, is found in the brains of mammals, like humans and other primates.

This area is responsible for things like problem solving, flexible thinking, self-awareness, and memory.

SKRT
SKRTCH
SKRTCH
SKRTCH

In other words...

...it's the intellectual powerhouse.

But birds don't have a PFC. Our brains are built totally differently from a mammal's brain.

So scientists used to believe that birds must act totally on pre-wired instincts, like robots, since they didn't have anything in their brain that would let them really "think."

SCRIBBLE

CREAK

Scientists realized the crows were using a part of their brain called the *nidopallium caudolaterale.*

Whoa.

Yeah. Let's just call it the NCL.

The PFC is in the neocortex—the folded outer layer of a mammal's brain—in the front, and the NCL is buried within a bird's pallium toward the back...but they do the same thing!

And guess which birds have the biggest NCL?

Umm...

Is it you?

?

Bingo!

WOW!

The forebrain—especially the NCL— in corvids, and some parrots, is bigger than in any other birds.

Crow

Pigeon

Now, some scientists think the number of neurons in the forebrain is important.

For example, an elephant brain has three times more neurons than a human brain.

But while elephants are smart, humans' intelligence is more advanced—and maybe that's because they have three times as many *forebrain* neurons.

256 Billion Neurons Total
250.4 billion   5.6 billion

86 Billion Neurons Total
70 billion   16 billion

So we might be able to measure intelligence partly by the number of neurons in the forebrain, where the PFC and NCL are found.

...and birds have really dense neurons!

Right you are! Good one, Buddy.

And since crows have such big forebrains, they can pack a whole lot of neurons in there.

WAG WAG

A crow's brain has as many neurons in the forebrain as some primates.

For example, a rook has slightly more forebrain neurons than a macaque, despite being 5 times smaller.

Rook   Brain Weight
        8.36 g

        Forebrain Neurons
        820 million

Macaque Brain Weight
        46.2 g

        Forebrain Neurons
        801 million

20

Ahem.

Of course, things like "neurons" and "nidopalliums" don't mean much if you don't put them to *use*.

And that...

...is what crows do best.

Humans have been watching us for a long time. And even if scientists didn't understand *how* crows were so smart...

...most people could see we were getting up to some pretty clever stuff.

One of Aesop's fables stars a thirsty crow and a pitcher of water. The crow discovered the water was too low to reach.

So the crow collected some stones...

...and dropped them into the pitcher to raise the water level.

In modern times, scientists have used the same setup to test the causal reasoning of crows and children.

They floated a reward on the surface of water in a beaker and provided a variety of objects to displace the water.

Corvus moneduloides / New Caledonian Crow

The crows preferred objects that were bigger...

...objects with more volume...

...and objects that sank instead of floated...

...to displace as much water as quickly as possible! The crows seemed to understand the properties of the objects and how they would affect the volume of water.

CHOMP

Children aged 4 to 8 were given the same task with sinking and floating objects.

Crows beat the 4-year-olds and had the same success as the 5-year-olds.

The older children performed better.

Crows will drop certain foods like clams and hard-shelled nuts onto hard surfaces to open them.

Bombs away!

But this isn't always a surefire method.

Open, dangit!

So sometimes we drop clams or nuts in front of the wheels of cars...

VrRRRRRR

...so the cars run over them and open them up.

Dead squirrels sometimes get the same treatment, since their skins are too tough for crow beaks to tear open.

Heave ho!

Some crows have perfected this technique.

They position themselves on wires above crosswalks to drop their walnuts.

They wait for the light to turn green...

...then collect their opened nuts when it's safe.

Safety first!

Impressive, *eh?*

Nuts aren't as tasty as kibble, either.

Well, *you're* a tough nut to crack, aren't you? The light's green now, by the way.

A Crow's Diet

What a crow eats partly depends on where it lives. In urban areas, human garbage is a perennial favorite for crows and usually makes up most of our diet.

But we still keep up a more traditional diet as well!

Some common foods are nuts and seeds,

fruits,

grains,

and eggs.

We get meat from invertebrates,

fish,

frogs and snakes,

and nestlings...

...and, of course, carrion!

Which, in settled areas, usually means roadkill.

38

The crows quickly learned which colors had food in them.

Nearly a year passed...

...and the crows still remembered which colors of bin held the food.

Too easy!

We have to have a good memory, not just to help us find food, but to remember where we cached it.

Cached it?

When an animal *caches* food, that means it's hiding it away to eat later.

Oh! I know this trick!

39

Species that tend to cache food have a large *hippocampus*.

It plays a big role in memory, including *spatial memory*.

For example: where we put things!

Hippocampus

Despite their smaller size, a nutcracker's hippocampus is larger than a crow's, since they need to keep track of those caches.

So can crows remember their hiding spots?

Or can't they?

Maybe this experiment will answer your question.

Crows were put in an aviary with over a thousand cache sites, and were allowed to hide their food.

Corvus brachyrhynchos
American Crow

Even after thirty days had passed, they remembered their caches with 80% accuracy— including which ones they'd already collected.

Cache

Collected last week

Cache

Nutcrackers, given a similar test, remembered 90% of their caches. Better than crows, but not by a huge amount.

So abandoning caches doesn't always mean we forget them... we just might not *need* them. And forgotten nuts and seeds can grow into new plants.

We can be choosy about what we cache, too. For example, we'll eat the biggest, most nutritious walnuts right away...

...and the inferior ones get saved for caching.

Rejects to be cached

45

You're a noble soul, Buddy. But most crows—and dogs, I bet—would munch it up once I was out of sight.

Crows steal from one another?

Let's just say we never turn down a free meal. So if you want to keep your food away from prying eyes and beaks, you have to play some *mind games*.

Some crows—most notably ravens and rooks—will watch another crow hiding food, take note of the location, and come back later to steal it.

So the bird caching the food will perform a bit of sleight of hand.

They *pretend* to hide their food...

♪

...then go hide it somewhere else while their rival is checking out the fake hiding spot.

?

Psych!

The question is, do crows really understand what their rival is *thinking?*

Or is moving food around when other crows are nearby just an instinct?

Corvus corax
Common Raven

To find an answer, scientists performed an experiment on ravens, expert sneaky cachers.

Here—they put two ravens in adjoining rooms with a peephole between them, like this.

SKRITCH SKRITCH

Those aren't ravens, Crow. Those are french fries.

Work with me, here, Buddy. You have to use your imagination.

Come to think of it, that's what this experiment is all about.

Imagination.

...it didn't bother guarding its caches, since the peephole was closed.

CROAK CROAK

But how did Raven A know it was safe from being watched if the peephole was closed, and unsafe if it was open...

SAFE! ✓ DANGER! ✗

...if it couldn't actually see a raven watching from the other side?

The researchers theorized it was using its *imagination*.

Raven A remembered the experience of watching Raven B through the peephole, and was now *imagining* that Raven B might be doing the same thing to them.

Scientists consider imagination, and being able to perceive the state of mind of other animals, to be very advanced forms of cognition.

They call this *theory of mind*, and most consider it to be unique to humans.

What are they thinking? Are they thinking about me?

There's the breeding pair—that's mom and dad. Those two mate for life.

Then there's the annual offspring...

...and then you've got the helpers.

"Helpers"? What do they help with?

They help raise the offspring.

That's known as *cooperative breeding*. American, carrion, and northwestern crows practice this...

...along with roughly half of the Corvidae family, particularly jays.

American Crow

Carrion Crow

Florida Scrub Jay

Pinyon Jay

Northwestern Crow

Black-Throated Magpie-Jay

In general, though, it's rare among birds. Only 9% of all bird species are known to breed cooperatively.

Non-cooperative
Cooperative

But research shows that birds that mate for life and breed cooperatively have larger brains than other birds.

Smallest Brain

Small Brain

Big Brain

Biggest Brain

Polyandrous (Female breeds with multiple males)

Polygynous (Male breeds with multiple females)

Long-Term (Mating for life)

Long-Term & Cooperative

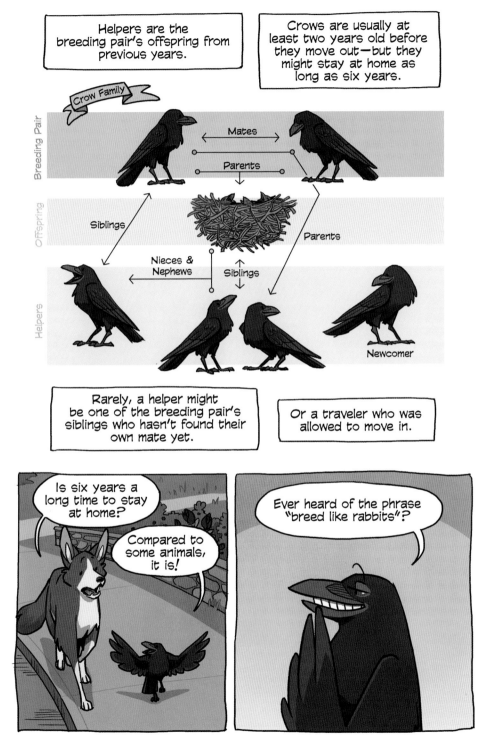

Helpers are the breeding pair's offspring from previous years.

Crows are usually at least two years old before they move out—but they might stay at home as long as six years.

Crow Family

Breeding Pair

Offspring

Helpers

Mates

Parents

Siblings

Parents

Nieces & Nephews

Siblings

Siblings

Newcomer

Rarely, a helper might be one of the breeding pair's siblings who hasn't found their own mate yet.

Or a traveler who was allowed to move in.

Is six years a long time to stay at home?

Compared to some animals, it is!

Ever heard of the phrase "breed like rabbits"?

Rabbits leave home when they're about 20 days old so their mother can start breeding again right away.

Rabbits add up *fast.*

And that's a good survival strategy: make a lot of babies!

Baby bunnies are so cute!

So scientists have wondered what the benefit of cooperative breeding is.

Wouldn't the species have a better chance at survival if young crows started breeding right away?

Wouldn't they?

Well, crows that stay at home longer can help make sure their siblings thrive.

Older sister

They may not be reproducing themselves, but they can increase the number of their parents' offspring that survive, by helping around the nest and protecting the territory.

And it's possible that a species that helps raise their siblings are practicing for raising their own kids so they'll be more successful parents. Basically, it's all a different kind of survival strategy!

PARENTING 101

You have to practice raising babies?

Nope! We don't *have* to.

Crows can leave home before becoming a helper, and once they're sexually mature—at about 3 years old—they can start a family with no experience.

Have you ever done this before?

Nope.

Me neither.

Family may still be close by, though, since crows often settle down near their parents.

Hi, Mom!

Stop by for dinner, honey!

Grown-up crows sometimes visit their parents or siblings and spend time together.

In the spring, the whole family helps gather nesting materials.

And once the female is incubating the eggs, everyone helps bring her food.

Everyone works together to keep predators away from the nest, too.

And to act as lookouts, defending the breeding pair's territory.

CAW!
CAW!
CAW!
CAW!

The eggs hatch after roughly 18 days.

Actual Size

Crows are *altricial*, meaning they're blind and helpless when they hatch.

Oh, that's why they're so ugly!

Whatever.

Precocial birds are able to walk and feed themselves as soon as they hatch—like chickens.

Let's go!

In late spring and early summer, crows fledge, meaning they leave the nest. They hang out in the trees, hopping and flapping from branch to branch as they build up the strength to fly.

But they can also fall to the ground before they've built up enough strength.

I saw a weird little crow in the bushes, one spring! I thought it fell out of its nest!

Watch who you're calling weird. *Yeesh.*

But...yeah, that was probably a fledgling. They *can* be a bit goofy looking.

Blue eyes

Inside of the mouth is red

Pink lips (gape)

Might still have some downy tufts

Feather sheathes may still be visible

They're defenseless on the ground before they can fly, but their parents will still try to protect them.

Oh! Is that who attacked me?

Yeah. Crows sometimes dive-bomb humans, too, if they get too close to fledglings.

CAW! CAW!

Eeek!

But they aren't trying to be vicious! They're just trying to protect their little ones.

In the fall, when fledglings have grown into juveniles, they get to meet more crows as different families start to mingle.

They join together, along with flocks of unmated birds, to form large foraging parties.

Winter is when the *really* big gatherings happen, though. Huge groups called *crow roosts* gather together at night.

Although some crows spend winter nights on their breeding territory, many choose to become part of these roosts.

Other members of a roost can be crows that have migrated south from colder climates or unmated wanderers.

From a local family | Migrating crow | Couple of strangers

In such large numbers, crows have a better chance of spotting predators.

CAW! CAW!

zzz...

Huh?!

CAW!

CAW!

CAW!

And when I say these roosts are huge, I mean *huge*. They can be up to 2 million birds strong!

Then, in spring...families head back to stay on their breeding territories.

Not all crows follow exactly the same social lifestyles, though. Jungle crows and common ravens are less social than American crows, for example.

And rooks breed in colonies, instead of on individual territories.

Don't live with extended family.

Everyone nests in the same area.

If young crows choose not to stay on with their family in the spring, they'll leave to go wandering, mingling with flocks of other unmated crows.

Travel safe!

They might wander for months to years before settling down with a fellow wanderer.

Some crows might even choose to return home to their parents again after wandering for a while.

I'm back!

That sort of sounds like my human family!

You're back!

Ha! Actually, crows do a lot of things that remind humans of themselves, since we're such social creatures.

But you have to be careful about assigning human emotions to crows. Even if we do things that remind humans of how they'd act, we might be doing them for different reasons.

Take *crow funerals*, for example.

What's a "crow funeral"? That sounds creepy.

That's what humans think, too.

Imagine this: there's a dead crow on the ground.

Then you hear a single crow cawing.

CAW! CAW!

And then some more.

CAW! CAW! CAW! CAW! CAW! CAW! CAW! CAW! CAW!

When crows gather around their dead, they check out the area so they can learn about any new dangers.

Any predator near the dead body will be associated with danger in the future.

= DANGER!

Wow. So even *dead* crows help out their family and friends.

I guess you could think of it that way.

And hey, here we are at the—

PARK!

And look! Crow friends!

Ugh! You're such a soft touch.

Grr!

BARK!

BARK!

?

?

What was that?!

That was me.

You can *bark?*

I can *mimic* all sorts of noises! Meow like a cat, bark like a dog— even talk like a human.

I thought all crows could say was "caw"!

No way.

Crows are *songbirds,* after all.

Really...?

Yup. We might not have the prettiest songs—but we do have a big repertoire!

Some birds have their calls hardwired into their brain. A chicken who never hears another chicken will still vocalize normally.

COCK-A-DOODLE-DOO!

But songbirds learn their calls. Most learn during childhood, but some songbirds can learn new songs throughout their lives.

Birds like mockingbirds, lyrebirds...and crows!

Mimus polyglottos / Northern Mockingbird

Menura novaehollandiae / Lyrebird

That's pretty important for social birds like crows, because different groups of crows have different *dialects*—unique songs.

These songs, sung softly and at close quarters, are made up of a variety of noises.

Coo-coo.

Squawk.

If an outsider wants to join a group, they have to listen and learn the dialect of the group in order to be accepted.

MEOW!

RING!

HONK!

BARK!

Is that why they attacked you?

Yeah. They realized I was a stranger.

So you barked to scare them away!

Yup. And that's mimicry.

Crows pick up all sorts of sounds to add to their vocabulary. Even human speech, if they hang around humans enough.

Usually crows who learn human speech have been kept in captivity.

It can be pretty startling to humans if these crow make it back into the wild.

Hello!

!

Especially since crows don't discriminate— they'll pick up naughty words, too.

$!/*#!

Well, generally, crows get along pretty swell, and most squabbles aren't serious. But we can get touchy about the boundaries of our territories.

Oh! That's what that "caw-caw" call is for!

You got it.

Even in winter, when crows roost communally, a breeding pair will check in on their territory during the day.

Territories can be a few square miles in the wild. But in cities, with so much food to go around, they can be much smaller.

But even a small territory is still a territory worth defending!

Wild crow's territory

Urban crow's territory (about a few house lots)

And even though play is rare in birds, with only 1% of bird species playing in even one of those three ways...

Birds who play!

Birds who don't

...crows engage in all three types of play. Maybe that's because play is more common in large-brained species!

And crows have big brains.

So true!

I've never seen a crow playing before today, though.

That might be because a big, scary dog could make a crow nervous, and nervous crows don't play.

Humans have noticed crows playing, though—in some very humanlike ways.

I'm not scary...

Crows have been seen appearing to snowboard down rooftops on plastic lids...

Corvus cornix / Hooded Crow

...and windsurf in updrafts using pieces of bark.

Corvus corax / Common Raven

Toolsh?

Tools— like that stick.

But shticks are for playing fetch.

It can be a tool, too!

Just ask a New Caledonian crow. They're stick whizzes... so scientists set up a test for them.

Corvus moneduloides
New Caledonian Crow

They put a piece of food out of reach in a glass case. There was a long stick that could reach it, but it was also out of reach, in a cage. A shorter stick hung from a branch.

Short stick

So what did the crows do?

Food

Glass case

Long stick

First, they hauled up the string until they got the short stick.

Then they used the short stick to fish the longer stick out of the cage.

Then they use the long stick to reach the food. Success!

But that wasn't the only impressive thing going on.

The crows had been trained earlier to understand that the short stick was too short to reach the food.

Well this is useless.

But they *still* retrieved it.

This suggests they had a multi-step mental plan before jumping into action.

I know this is useless to reach the food, but if I can reach the longer stick...

And to pull off something like *that*, you need a good *working memory*.

What's that?

"Working memory" is what you use to keep track of multiple pieces of information while you're in the middle of doing something.

TAP TAP

Without it, you couldn't keep track of what you were saying, reading, or thinking.

You couldn't work through a math problem.

It's also what crows and primates relied on in those image and number matching games.

In fact, crows have been shown to have a working memory as advanced as primates!

But New Caledonian crows don't just use tools in fancy experiments in labs. They use them in the wild, too—in fact, they *make* them.

And since humans and primates rely on their prefrontal cortex for their working memory...

...4, 5, 6.

...in crows, it's another job for our big honkin' NCL.

Stepped tools are cut out of pandanus leaves.

Hooked tools are made by cutting down twigs.

Both are used for fishing grubs out of tree trunks.

SNip RIP RIP RIP RIP SNIP

SNIP SNIP SNIP SNIP

This is made easier by the New Caledonian crow's anatomy. They have better binocular vision than other crows—that's the area in front of you that both eyes can see.

61.5° 42.0°

New Caledonian Crow | American Crow

Also, most crows' bills are slightly hooked at the end, but the New Caledonian's is straight, making it easier to hold a tool straight out in front of them where they can see it.

New Caledonian Crow | American Crow

So they're pretty special crows!

On top of that, making hooked tools is very rare.

The fact is, the only animals aside from crows that are known to make their own hooked tools are humans.

That's... pretty rare.

The hooked-tool-making club!

Yup, it's a two-animal club!

90

Beyond that, only a small handful of animals are known to make more than one kind of tool like the New Caledonian crows: capuchin monkeys, orangutans, chimpanzees, and humans.

That's still a pretty exclusive club!

The multi-tool-making club!

So since New Caledonian crows are so clever about tools, scientists gave them another test—this time, a tool-making test.

They were given a straight wire and shown a small bucket with a piece of meat in it at the bottom of a tube.

The crows bent the wire by pushing it against the beaker...

...and fished out the bucket.

Hooded crows and common ravens use the lines at ice-fishing holes to pull up fish.

American crows have used stone hammers to open acorns...

...used cups to transport water...

...and chiseled down splinters of wood with their beaks to use as probing tools.

You can think of the stones rooks use to displace water and the cars carrion crows use to open walnuts as tools, too.

CRACK!

Still, New Caledonian crows definitely make and use tools more often than other crows. They're the tool-making experts!

Why don't other crows use tools more often if they *can?*

It doesn't make as much sense for us.

New Caledonian crows evolved on islands with few predators, and with no woodpeckers to compete with for those grubs in the wood. So they can safely take the time to make and use tools.

Other crows don't have those luxuries, and can usually get their food without tools, anyway.

But sometimes, if the situation demands it, they can innovate tool use.

And that's a real show of intelligence, in any crow—

—the ability to size up a problem and think of how to use tools in a completely new way to solve it.

But my humans aren't *dangerous!* They protect me and look after me!

Well, you're their pet, after all.

But it's illegal to own crows as pets in the United States and Canada, under the *Migratory Bird Treaty Act.*

What's that?

It's a set of laws meant to stop people from hunting, capturing, or selling native birds.

It was established after a number of birds were hunted to extinction, or near extinction, in the 1800s, in part because feathers were popular as hat decorations.

But the treaty has exceptions. For example, it's legal to hunt crows in lots of places, either for sport or if they're being pests.

BLAM!

WAG WAG

You're not a pest, Crow!

Thanks, but...

...some humans might not like their garbage bins being raided.

...Oh. Right.

And in agricultural areas, crows eat some of the corn and other crops. So farmers don't like us much.

But then again, we also eat lots of insects that damage crops.

European Corn Borer

People also hunt us because they think crows destroy other birds' populations by eating eggs and nestlings.

Yum!

But crows are a less common nest predator than other animals.

Yum!

CAW! CAW! CAW!
CAW! CAW! CAW!
CAW!
CAW!

And then there's the big—literally big— problem of crow roosts. They can make a lot of noise and leave behind a mess of droppings.

CAW! CAW! CAW! CAW!

Humans have gone to extreme measures to break up roosts. In 1940 in Rockford, Illinois, dynamite was used to kill over 300,000 crows while they roosted.

CAW!
CAW!
CAW!
CAW!
CAW!
CAW!
CAW!
BOOM

But it's not just the nitty-gritty stuff about destruction and dirt. Crows just have a really bad rap in general.

Ever heard of a "murder of crows"?

What's that?

It's a poetic way of referring to a flock of crows, first recorded over 600 years ago, in the 15th century.

A Murther of Crowes

It was a *term of venery* — a hunting term used by aristocrats.

Maybe it was coined because crows eat dead bodies—including those on medieval battlefields and during the plague.

Whatever the reason, the name has stuck—and people still associate us with death.

Do all humans hate crows?

Well... not *all* humans.

And that can be confusing for a crow. Some humans will tolerate us in their yards—others will shoot us on sight.

When opinions on crows shift so much between different humans, crows have to be smart and adaptable, with good memories, to live alongside them.

Who's dangerous? Who's safe?

Lucky for us, we can recognize individual humans.

In fact, an experiment using masks was carried out in Seattle to study how well wild crows could distinguish faces, and what they could do with this information.

Corvus brachyrhynchos
American Crow

The researchers had two types of masks—the "dangerous" masks resembling cavemen and the "neutral" masks of famous politicians.

Neutral →

← Dangerous

Wearing the dangerous mask, they caught and banded wild crows.

Eek! Let me go, you thug!

After the crows were released, researchers walked around wearing the "neutral" mask. The crows ignored them.

A few days later, they walked around wearing the "dangerous" mask again...

...and several of the crows covered them in verbal abuse.

CAW! CAW! CAW! CAW! CAW!

The researchers continued to wear the two masks. The neutral mask was ignored, but a growing number of crows would scold and mob the dangerous mask.

CAW!

CAW!

CAW!

CAW!

CAW!

Even those who hadn't been banded.

And over the years, the next generations also learned about the dangerous mask.

It's been over a decade now, and these crows are still learning from one another.

CAW! CAW!

CAW!

The moral of this story is: watch out if you cross a crow. We know how to hold a grudge.

It's a good thing I'm not a human!

Oh, we recognize individual dogs, too.

!

With so many crows living alongside humans in urban areas, there are lots of opportunities for people to observe crows. And while some people still find them noisy, annoying, and even ominous...

CAW!
CAW!

CAW!

CAW! CAW!

...others find their behavior really fascinating.

One hand-raised crow in the city of Vancouver rose to global fame after stealing a knife from a crime scene. And people did make a lot of murder-related jokes...

DO NOT CRO

...but Canuck the Crow has since grown a huge social media following, allowing people to discover just how sociable and clever crows can be.

SNAP! SNAP! SNAP!
SNAP! SNAP!
SNAP! SNAP!
SNAP!

Other people take things a step further by trying to befriend crows themselves, leaving out food for them.

—GLOSSARY—

Altricial

Born or hatched naked and blind. Altricial animals can't care for themselves right away.

Caching

Hiding food to eat at a later time.

Carnivores

Animals whose main source of food is meat.

Cone Cells

Cells in the eyes that receive light. Signals from these cells are translated by the brain into color.

Cooperative Breeding

Offspring are raised both by parents and by additional group members, or helpers.

Corvidae

A family of birds to which crows belong. Any bird in this family is called a corvid.

Corvus

A genus of the family Corvidae that includes crows, ravens, and rooks.

Crow Funerals

The behavior of crows to gather en masse around a dead crow.

Crow Roosts

A place where crows gather together in large numbers to spend the night during the fall and winter.

Crows

May refer collectively to birds in the family Corvidae, or more specifically to a species in the *Corvus* genus.

Encephalization Quotient
A way of measuring relative brain size based on the difference between an animal's actual brain size and the predicted brain size for their body. Called the EQ for short.

Fledgling
A young bird who's just fledged, or left the nest.

Forebrain
A large part of the brain, the functions of which include thinking, perceiving, language, and memory.

Helpers
In cooperative breeding, helpers are non-parental family members who assist in raising the offspring.

Hippocampus
A structure in the brain that helps keep track of spatial memory and long-term memory.

Locomotor Play
A type of play in animals that involves moving one's own body, such as rolling down a hill.

Migratory Bird Treaty Act
A set of laws that prohibit people from hunting native birds for profit, e.g., to sell them as pets or sell their feathers. It also makes it illegal to keep native birds as pets.

Mimicry
The imitation of something. Crows can mimic sounds they hear with great accuracy.

Neuron
A type of cell in the nervous system that transmits information.

—GLOSSARY CONTINUED—

Nidopallium Caudolaterale
> A structure in a bird's brain that is involved in complex thinking. Called the NCL for short.

Object Play
> A type of play in animals that involves using an object, such as rolling a ball.

Omnivores
> Animals that eat both plant matter and meat.

Precocial
> Born or hatched in a mature state with fur or feathers. Precocial animals can move around shortly after birth.

Prefrontal Cortex
> A structure in a mammal's brain that is involved in complex thinking. Called the PFC for short.

Social Play
> A type of play in animals that involves interaction with another animal, such as tug-of-war.

Spatial Memory
> A type of memory to keep track of where things are.

Term of Venery
> A fanciful way to refer to a gathering of animals of the same species, invented by hunters in the Middle Ages. "A murder of crows" is a term of venery.

Theory of Mind
> The understanding that other people have thoughts and feelings separate from our own.

Working Memory
> A type of short-term memory that holds on to different pieces of information we need while completing a task.

—NOTES—

Page 7: Crows have been seen using tools in amazing ways, many described in this book, but it should be noted that no one has actually seen a crow propping open a pet flap with a stick . . . yet.

Page 52: While it's true most crow species are flourishing, there are some exceptions. The Hawaiian crow is extinct in the wild, with only a few birds left living in captivity, and the Mariana crow is critically endangered. These species live on small, isolated islands and so have been vulnerable to habitat loss and to predators introduced by humans. Conservation efforts are in progress for both species.

Page 76: Experiments carried out in captivity showed that an outsider crow would be shunned or chased away by an established group. It was theorized that this is because the outsider had different short-range calls; as they began imitating the calls of the group, they became accepted.

Page 77: Although scientists suspect the number of crow calls hold some meaning, they haven't yet figured out what those meanings are. That's one crow code we're still trying to crack!

LIVING WITH CROWS 101

I found a baby crow on the ground! Should I help it?

The parents are probably nearby, and it's best for fledglings to stay with their family, so you should leave it where it is. But you can gently pick it up and place it on a low branch if you think it's in danger.

If it's obviously injured or can't perch on a branch, contact your local wildlife rehabilitation center and ask for their advice. Remember that it's illegal for anyone other than a certified rehabilitator to raise crows.

Older nestlings may look like fledglings, but they're not strong enough yet to perch on branches.

Fledglings hop around and can perch on branches. Leave them alone unless they're injured.

Help! Crows keep dive-bombing me!

Is it fledging season? If so, the attacks will stop once the fledglings have learned to fly! If it keeps happening in the same area, try avoiding it for a few days or using an umbrella.

If it's a more lasting grudge, you can try to turn their opinion of you around by befriending them. Drop food behind you when you're out walking around. They may focus on the food instead of their vendetta and learn to associate you with good things, instead.

A trail of peanuts is a nice distraction!

How do I get crows to bring me gifts?

Gift-giving can certainly seem like an intentional token of appreciation, but scientists aren't sure what crows are thinking when they leave these "gifts" behind. It may be that they happen to be carrying something in their beak, then drop it to pick up food at a feeder.

It will most likely be a one-time occurence, but if it leads to more food being left out, clever crows may learn to associate leaving trinkets with being fed. Whatever the case is, the best way to receive a gift from crows is by feeding them regularly. Just know that gifting is rare!

What should I feed crows?

Crows eat discarded junk food because it's easily available, and, hey, a crow's gotta take what it can get! But that doesn't mean it's the healthiest food for us, so it's best to leave it off the menu. Unsalted peanuts—shelled or unshelled— are a great choice, as well as fruit, eggs, and scraps of meat.

And don't be surprised if your birdbath gets used as a food-soaking station—crows are sometimes known to moisten their food with water, particularly if they're taking it home to feed their young.

—BOOKS—

Emery, N. (2016). *Bird Brain: An Exploration of Avian Intelligence.* Princeton University Press.

Herculano-Houzel, S. (2016). *The Human Advantage: A New Understanding of How Our Brain Became Remarkable.* MIT Press.

Lipton, J. (1993). *An Exaltation of Larks: The Ultimate Edition.* Penguin Group USA.

Marzluff, J. M., & Angell, T. (2007). *In the Company of Crows and Ravens.* Yale University Press.

Marzluff, J. M., & Angell, T. (2013). *Gifts of the Crow: How Perception, Emotion, and Thought Allow Smart Birds to Behave like Humans.* Simon and Schuster.

Turner, P. (2016). *Crow Smarts: Inside the Brain of the World's Brightest Bird.* HMH Books for Young Readers.

—ARTICLES & WEB SOURCES—

Balakhonov, D., & Rose, J. (2017). "Crows Rival Monkeys in Cognitive Capacity." *Scientific Reports*, vol. 7, no. 1.

Bogale, B. A., et al. (2012). "Long-Term Memory of Color Stimuli in the Jungle Crow (*Corvus macrorhynchos*)." *Animal Cognition*, vol. 15, no. 2.

Boswall, J. (1977 & 1978). "Tool-Using by Birds and Related Behaviour." *Aviculture Magazine*, vol. 83 & 84.

Boswall, J. (1983). "Tool-Using and Related Behaviour in Birds: More Notes." *Avicultural Magazine*, vol. 89, no. 2.

Bugnyar, T., et al. (2016). "Ravens Attribute Visual Access to Unseen Competitors." *Nature Communications*, vol. 7.

Caccamise, D. F., et al. (1997). "Roosting Behavior and Group Territoriality in American Crows." *The Auk*, vol. 114, no. 4.

Caffrey, C. (2000). "Tool Modification and Use by an American Crow." *The Wilson Bulletin*, vol. 112, no. 2.

Cristol, D. A. (2001). "American Crows Cache Less Preferred Walnuts." *Animal Behaviour*, vol. 62, no. 2.

Cross, D. J., et al. (2013). "Distinct Neural Circuits Underlie Assessment of a Diversity of Natural Dangers by American Crows." *Proceedings of the Royal Society B: Biological Sciences*, vol. 280, no. 1765.

Dally, J. M., et al. (2006). "The Behaviour and Evolution of Cache Protection and Pilferage." *Animal Behaviour*, vol. 72, no. 1.

Ditz, H. M., & Nieder, A. (2015). "Neurons Selective to the Number of Visual Items in the Corvid Songbird Endbrain." *Proceedings of the National Academy of Sciences*, vol. 112, no. 25.

Emery, N. J., & Clayton, N. S. (2004). "The Mentality of Crows: Convergent Evolution of Intelligence in Corvids and Apes." *Science*, vol. 306, no. 5703.

Emery, N. J., et al. (2007). "Cognitive Adaptations of Social Bonding in Birds." *Philosophical Transactions of the Royal Society B: Biological Sciences*, vol. 362, no. 1480.

Goldsmith, T. H. (2006). "What Birds See." *Scientific American*, vol. 295, no. 1.

Griesser, M., & Suzuki, T. N. (2016). "Occasional Cooperative Breeding in Birds and the Robustness of Comparative Analyses Concerning the Evolution of Cooperative Breeding." *Zoological Letters*, vol. 2, no. 1.

Jelbert, S. A., et al. (2015). "Investigating Animal Cognition with the Aesop's Fable Paradigm: Current Understanding and Future Directions." *Communicative & Integrative Biology*, vol. 8, no. 4.

Lefebvre, L., et al. (1997). "Feeding Innovations and Forebrain Size in Birds." *Animal Behaviour*, vol. 53, no. 3.

Lefebvre, L., et al. (2002). "Tools and Brains in Birds." *Behaviour*, vol. 139, no. 7.

Marzluff, J. M., et al. (2001). "Causes and Consequences of Expanding American Crow Populations." In *Avian Ecology and Conservation in an Urbanizing World*. Springer, Boston, MA.

McGowan, K. J. (2010). "Frequently Asked Questions about Crows." Retrieved from birds.cornell.edu/crows/crowfaq.htm

Olkowicz, S., et al. (2016). "Birds Have Primate-Like Numbers of Neurons in the Forebrain." *Proceedings of the National Academy of Sciences*, vol. 113, no. 26.

RT. (2012, January 12). "Crowboarding: Russian Roof-Surfin' Bird Caught on Tape" [Video file]. Retrieved from youtube.com/watch?v=3dWw9GLcOeA

Rutz, C., et al. (2016). "Tool Bending in New Caledonian Crows." *Royal Society Open Science*, vol. 3, no. 8.

Swift, K. N., & Marzluff, J. M. (2015). "Wild American Crows Gather Around Their Dead to Learn about Danger." *Animal Behaviour*, vol. 109.

Taylor, A. H., et al. (2010). "Complex Cognition and Behavioural Innovation in New Caledonian Crows." *Proceedings of the Royal Society B: Biological Sciences*, vol. 277, no. 1694.

Thompson, F. R. (2007). "Factors Affecting Nest Predation on Forest Songbirds in North America." *Ibis*, vol. 149.

Troscianko, J., et al. (2012). "Extreme Binocular Vision and a Straight Bill Facilitate Tool Use in New Caledonian Crows." *Nature Communications*, vol. 3.

Veit, L., & Nieder, A. (2013). "Abstract Rule Neurons in the Endbrain Support Intelligent Behaviour in Corvid Songbirds." *Nature Communications*, vol. 4.

Verbeek, N. A., & Caffrey, C. (2002). "American Crow (*Corvus brachyrhynchos*)," *The Birds of North America* (A. F. Poole and F. B. Gill, Eds.). Ithaca: Cornell Lab of Ornithology. Retrieved from birdsna.org/Species-Account/bna/species/amecro

Weir, A. A., et al. (2002). "Shaping of Hooks in New Caledonian Crows." *Science*, vol. 297, no. 5583.